WITH A WIG WITH A WAG

and other American folk tales

Edited by JEAN COTHRAN

Illustrated by CLIFFORD N. GEARY

DAVID McKAY COMPANY, Inc. New York,

Typography by Charles M. Todd

To

MOTHER AND DAD

🕸 *Acknowledgments* 🕸

For permission to reprint, adapt or retell the stories listed below, the editor is indebted to:

The American Folklore Society, for the following:

From the *Journal of American Folklore:*

"With a Wig, With a Wag," a retelling of "The Three Brothers and the Hag," from *English Folk-Tales in America*, by L. Conant, Vol. VIII (1895), "Old Bluebeard," from *Mountain White Folk-lore: Tales of the Southern Blue Ridge*, recorded by Isabel Gordon Carter, Vol. XXXVIII (1925); "Mister Deer's My Riding Horse," a retelling of one of the *Two Negro Tales*, recorded by Mrs. William Preston Johnston, Vol. IX (1896); "Coyote and the Alder Stump," a retelling of "Coyote and the Stump," #5 in *A Study of Wintu Mythology* by D. Demetracopoulou and Cora du Bois, Vol. XLV (1932); "Little Bear," a retelling of "The Bear-Maiden," recorded by Albert Ernest Jenks, Vol. XV (1902).

From the *Memoirs of the American Folklore Society:*

"Mister Honey Mouth," a retelling of "The Elephant and the Whale," from *Louisiana Folk-Tales*, collected by Alcée

ACKNOWLEDGMENTS

Fortier, Vol. II (1895), published for the Society by Houghton, Mifflin and Company; "The Cat, the Cock and the Lamb," a free translation by Inez Symington of "El Gato, El Gallito y El Borreguito," in *Spanish Folk-Tales from New Mexico*, by José Manuel Espinosa, Vol. XXX (1937); "The Singing Geese," from *Folklore from Maryland*, collected by Annie Weston Whitney and Caroline Canfield Bullock, Vol. XVIII (1925).

F. F. Latta, for "The Indian Shinny Game," a retelling of "Mih-kit-tee and Coo-choon the Crow," from *California Indian Folklore*, by F. F. Latta, published by the author, Shafter, California, 1936. Used and retold by permission of the author.

Charles Scribner's Sons, for "Stealing the Springtime," from *Kootenai Why Stories*, by Frank B. Linderman; copyright 1926 by Charles Scribner's Sons; 1954 by Norma Linderman Waller. Used by permission of the publishers.

University of California Press, for "The Old Woman and the Bear," from *Six California Tales*, by Burton Lowrimore; California Folklore Quarterly, Vol. IV (1945) P. 157. Used by permission of the University of California Press.

University of Michigan Press, for "Rusty Jack," from *Folklore from the Schoharie Hills, New York*, by Emelyn Elizabeth Gardner; University of Michigan Press, 1937. Used by permission of the University of Michigan Press.

❧ *Contents* ❦

CONTENTS

x

WITH A WIG, WITH A WAG

and other American folk tales

✎ *With A Wig, With A Wag* ✎

ONCE THERE WERE THREE BROTHERS WHO HAD NOT so much as a penny between them. When the daffodils began to dance, the eldest brother said, "I'm off to try my fortune."

And away he went. He traveled about for a long time until he saw a little white house. Walking up boldly, he knocked on the door. An old hag with two beady eyes and a tight pursed mouth cracked it open.

"May I stay the night?" asked the eldest brother, for the shadows were getting long.

"Yes," allowed the hag. "Come in."

And she showed him the ladder to her loft. Climbing up, he found a straw mat near the chimney and fell asleep. Towards the middle of the night a clinking noise woke him. He crept slowly to a knothole where a chink of light showed through. Putting his eye to the hole, he saw the old hag before a little fire counting piles of money. When she finished, she put the coins in a long leather bag and hung it on a hook in her cupboard. Then she fell asleep on the warm hearthstone.

When the eldest brother heard her snoring, he climbed carefully down the ladder, opened the cupboard, shouldered the leather bag and was off out the door. He never stopped running till he came to an old meetinghouse.

The meetinghouse asked, "Will you sweep me, lad?"

"No," answered the eldest brother. "I've no time to stop." And he took to his legs again.

As the sun came up, he passed by a field.

"Boy, will you weed me?" asked the field.

"Certainly not," said the eldest brother, and he was

2

off again, but not so briskly, for it seemed as though the bag had doubled in weight.

Soon he came to a well. As he stopped for a drink, the well asked, "Will you clean me, boy?"

"No," answered the brother without a second thought. "I've no time for that." On he went, the coins clinking at his side.

At noon he came to a meadow with a maple tree. In the maple's shade he sat down to rest.

Now when the old hag woke and found that both her treasure and the boy in the loft had disappeared, she put two and two together and reached for her birch rod. Then she was off down the road like a gust of March wind.

Going by the meetinghouse, she stopped to ask:

> Have you seen a lad
> With a wig, with a wag,
> With a long leather bag,
> Who stole all the money
> Ever I had?

The meetinghouse replied, "With a wig, with a wag, he came by here on his way to a field."

The old hag went on and came to the field.

3

Have you seen a lad
With a wig, with a wag,
With a long leather bag,
Who stole all the money
Ever I had?

"With a wig, with a wag, he came by here on his way to a well," replied the field.

The old hag scurried on again and came to the well.

Have you seen a lad
With a wig, with a wag,
With a long leather bag,
Who stole all the money
Ever I had?

"With a wig, with a wag, he's in yonder meadow under the maple tree," said the well.

On she went and came to the meadow. There was the eldest brother asleep under the tree. With a blow of the birch rod she did for the boy, then picked up the bag and started for home.

After some time the second brother said, "I'm off to seek my fortune." And away he went before ever the sun was up. He traveled until he too came to the old hag's house and knocked on the door.

"May I stay the night?" asked the second brother.

"Yes," allowed the crone. "Come in." And she showed him the ladder to the loft. He found the mat

4

by the chimney and quickly fell asleep. Waking in the middle of the night, he crept to the knothole and saw the old hag playing with her coins.

When the second brother heard her snoring, he climbed carefully down, found the leather bag and was off out the door.

"Will you sweep me, lad?" asked the meetinghouse as he hurried by.

"No," answered the second brother.

"Will you weed me, lad?" asked the field.

"No time to stop," said the boy.

"Will you clean me, lad?" asked the well.

"No time for that," repeated the second brother, the coins clinking at his side. On he ran until, like his eldest brother, he too fell asleep under the maple tree.

When the old crone found her bag and lodger gone for the second time, she whirled down the road like an angry wasp. The meetinghouse and the field and the well told her where the second brother had gone. Finding him, like the first, asleep under the tree, she finished off the second brother with her birch rod, picked up her bag and started for home.

Now when the youngest brother grew tired of living by himself, he too decided to seek his fortune. So one morning when the sun smiled over the hill, he

5

started on his way. He traveled about for a long time and finally came to the house of the old hag.

Yes, he might stay the night, and she showed him the ladder to the loft. Quickly he fell asleep, and when the clinking coins woke him, he crept to the knothole and saw the old crone stacking her money. After she went to sleep, he too found the bag and was off out the door. One foot before the other, he came to the meetinghouse.

"Will you sweep me, lad?"

Now the youngest brother always had been one to help his neighbors, so he answered, "Yes." And though it took a long time, he left no dust in the corners.

Then he ran till he came to the field.

"Will you weed me, lad?"

"Yes," answered the third brother. And furrow by furrow he pulled the weeds.

Then he went on till he came to the well.

"Will you clean me, lad?"

And though he was afraid the old woman surely would catch up with him, he cleaned it with care.

At noon he came to the maple tree and sat down to get his breath.

When the old hag awoke and found both treasure and lodger gone for the third time, she was off down the road like a streak of summer lightning.

6

Going by the meetinghouse, she asked:
> Have you seen a lad
> With a wig, with a wag,
> With a long leather bag,
> Who stole all the money
> Ever I had?

The meetinghouse made no answer. In a sudden whirl of wind, shingles from its roof blew every which way, and hitting the old hag, almost killed her.

She hurried on to the field.

> Have you seen a lad
> With a wig, with a wag,
> With a long leather bag,
> Who stole all the money
> Ever I had?

The field replied with a cloud of dust and stones which covered the old hag and almost blinded her. She hastened on to the well.

> Have you seen a lad
> With a wig, with a wag,
> With a long leather bag,
> Who stole all the money
> Ever I had?

Then the water in the well began to rise and overflow, and reaching out its cold arms, pulled her down its shaft.

The youngest brother went merrily home. Sharing his treasure with friends, he lived to a ripe old age.

Rusty Jack

ONCE UPON A TIME THERE LIVED A RICH FARMER WHO had three sons. The two older boys, James and Mark, were thrifty, hard-working lads; but the youngest, Rusty Jack, as he was called because he wore such old and rusty clothes, was neither so strong nor so good-looking as his brothers. So he was laughed at by them and considered a trial by his father. When the father came to die, he left all his houses and lands to James and Mark; while to Rusty Jack he left nothing but a good-for-nothing old ox, just ready to die.

Sure enough, the day after the father's funeral, when Rusty Jack went out to the barn to feed his ox, he found it lying dead. James and Mark laughed at him about his luck, and told him they now thought it was time that he set about earning his own living. How he was to do this Rusty Jack did not know, for he had never done a day's work in his life.

9

But he knew he could no longer stay at home; so he skinned his ox, hung the skin over his shoulder, and set out in his rusty old clothes to seek his fortune. Near sundown he became so tired that he felt he could not go another step; so he lay down to rest on the ground beside the road, throwing over him the oxhide, with the flesh side outside.

He was just about to fall asleep when a loud cawing

above his head startled him; and before he could raise himself up, a flock of crows alighted upon the hide and fell to pecking the raw meat. They all did this but one, which cocked his head on one side, and looking at Jack, cried, "Hello, Jack! Hello, Jack!" Then Rusty Jack knew that he had found a pet crow which he had lost more than a year before. The crow was as glad to see Jack as Jack was to find the crow; and when Jack put out his hand, calling, "Hello! Come to Jack!" the crow allowed himself to be caught.

Jack was so overjoyed at finding his pet that he forgot all about his aches and pains. He put a cord about the crow's leg, perched him on one shoulder, threw the oxhide over the other, and again set forth in search of his fortune. Presently, coming to a woodchopper's hut in the midst of a forest, he saw a bright light shining from one of the windows and peeped in. There, before the fireplace, he saw a table set with delicious meats, cakes, wine, and honey; and, more than that, at the table sat two women eating. One looked as though she might be the woodchopper's wife; but the other was a wonderfully beautiful young lady, with long golden hair, and jewels about her neck—a princess, maybe. Jack couldn't imagine who she could be, but thought that he had never before seen anyone half so beautiful.

As he stood gazing, he forgot all about the crow; and

the crow, not liking that, called out, "Jack, Jack!"
That frightened the women so, they snatched the food
off the table and threw it, tablecloth and all, into a chest
which stood in one corner of the room. Then they took
a big crock which stood near the fireplace, and removing
a few bricks from the floor, placed the crock in a hole
which seemed to have been made for it. Quickly replac-
ing the bricks, the beautiful young lady concealed her-
self under the valance of the bed which stood in a corner
of the room. The woodchopper's wife flew about, putting on the table mush and milk for her husband's supper, then disappeared up the ladder which led to the
loft.

Jack was so hungry that he thought he would go
in and help himself to the food in the chest; but before
he had time to get anything out, the woodchopper came
in.

"Whom have we here?" cried he, amazed, as he
saw a stranger making himself at home in his hut.

"Nobody but a poor hungry traveler," replied Jack.

"Well, if you are so hungry, draw up and have
some mush and milk with me," said the man. "You
have a tame crow there, I see. Does he happen to be
a talking crow?"

"That he does," answered Jack, a bright idea coming
into his head. "Hello!" he said to the bird.

12

"Hello, Jack!" croaked the crow.

The woodchopper was delighted. "Can he say any-thing else?" he asked.

"Oh yes!" said Jack. "He is a fortune-telling crow. Tell the woodchopper what is in yonder chest." With that, Jack pinched one of the crow's toes, whereupon the poor bird cried out, "Caw, caw, caw!"

"He says there is meat and cake and wine and honey in the chest," explained Jack.

The woodchopper laughed. "Why, how can that be, when we are so poor we hardly have enough to eat?"

"I don't know," said Jack, "but my crow always speaks the truth. You had better look and see."

So the woodchopper went to the chest and lifted the cover and peeped in. To his amazement, he found it just as the crow had said. After he had lifted out the good things, he and Jack feasted as they had never done before, and when they had eaten all they could hold, the woodchopper said:

"I should like your bird to tell me some other piece of good news. Can he?"

"I think so," answered Jack. "I think he can tell you where a treasure lies hidden, if you will agree to give me half of it."

"I'll do that," laughed the woodchopper, never

13

dreaming that the crow knew any more about where a treasure lay buried than he did.

Thereupon Jack again tweaked the crow's toe; and again the crow squawked, "Caw, caw, caw!"

"He says," explained Jack, "that if you will take up the nine bricks before the middle of the fireplace, you will find a treasure crock."

"A treasure crock!" shouted the woodchopper. "What on earth is that? How could there be any treasure buried before the fireplace when I laid every brick with my own hands?"

"But why not look?" asked Jack. "I've never known my crow to tell a lie." And after a little Jack persuaded the woodchopper to lift up the bricks. Sure enough, there was a huge crock. His hands trembled so, he could hardly lift the cover off; but when he did, such a sight as met his eyes! Jewels, gold and silver trinkets, and gold coin! More than the woodchopper had believed existed in the whole world.

"There!" exclaimed Jack. "Will you believe my crow next time?"

"I will; and I will give you my half of the treasure for him. Then I can go on finding other fortunes."

"Oh, I couldn't sell him," said Jack, "for I expect him to find me a wife and to earn enough to take care of us both; but I have left outside an oxhide which will

14

be worth much more to you than the crow. It was with that I caught him from out a whole flock of talking crows. All you have to do is to lie down beside the

road and throw the hide over you, flesh side outside, and more fortune-telling crows will alight on you than you will know what to do with. Then you can make them find fortunes for you and sell them for great sums of money."

"So I could," said the woodchopper. "I'll give you my half of the treasure for the hide."

Then Jack filled his pockets with his riches and tied the rest into his big pocket handkerchief. "Now," he

15

said to the crow, "before I go further, I am rich enough to marry me a wife. Where is there a beautiful lady who will marry me?" Again he pinched the crow's toe; and again the bird squawked, "Caw, caw, caw!"

"He says under the valance of the kitchen bed," explained Jack.

"That's a lie," said the woodchopper; but just the same he looked under the bed and sure enough, there was a beautiful young lady.

"Come out, come out!" coaxed Rusty Jack. "And I will marry you."

"Oh, will you?" cried the young lady. "That's what I've been looking for—a husband. The robbers came to my father's house and killed my father and brothers; and I barely managed to escape with a little of my father's wealth, on one of his horses. If you will go back with me and help me to bury my father and brothers, I will marry you and give you my father's large estate."

"With all my heart will I do that! And we'll keep the crow, for he will be able to get us out of any trouble we may get into."

By this time the woodchopper's wife came down from the loft; and they all had supper together, Jack and the woodchopper eating as though they had eaten nothing for a year.

In the morning Jack and the beautiful young lady set out to visit her father's estate and to bury her father and brothers; while the woodchopper started in the opposite direction with the oxhide, to procure for himself a flock of talking crows.

⊗ *A Dozen Is Thirteen* ⊗

ON THE LAST NIGHT OF THE YEAR 1654, THE GOOD baker, Boss Jan Pietersen Van Amsterdam, was keeping watch in his shop up the Hudson. All day his sales had been brisk. There had been a great demand for New Year's cakes, which he had invented, and gingerbread babies in the likeness of his own fat offspring. Tomorrow, to celebrate the holiday, everyone would want his olie-kocks and steaming mince pies. Yes, it had been a good year. He hoped the next would be as prosperous.

Then as midnight drew near, Boss Jan started to fidget. Stanch churchman though he was, the bane of his life was the fear of being bewitched. On this night he was always frightened lest evil spirits might make one final effort to claim him for their own.

Listening to the clock's relentless *tick-tock, tick-tock, tick-tock*, he was startled by a sharp rap on the door. An ugly old hag hobbled in, a shawl over her head half-

18

covering her shoe-button eyes and long hooked nose.

Banging on the counter, she cried in a shrill voice, "Give me a dozen New Year's cookies."

"You needn't speak so loud," answered Boss Jan, rousing himself from his reverie, "I'm not deaf." And he counted out a dozen cookies.

"A dozen," she screamed, "give me a dozen. Here are only twelve."

"Twelve is a dozen."

"One more. I want a dozen."

The lateness of the hour and his own dark thoughts were too much for Boss Jan's usually placid temper.

"Well, then," he snapped, "if you want another, go to the devil and get it."

The clock struck twelve as the old hag left the bake-shop and disappeared into the night.

Did she take him at his word? Boss Jan wondered.

From that hour, bad luck followed his steps until it seemed as though he were indeed bewitched. His cakes were stolen. His bread was so light that it went up the chimney, if it was not so heavy that it fell through the oven, and his children were always ill.

One day when the rest of the world was as gay as the blooming tulips, Boss Jan sat brooding in his shop. Suddenly a thundershower broke overhead. Great flashes of lightning streaked the darkened sky, and the bolts rumbled like ninepins down some cloud-hidden alley. A gusty wind blew open the bakeshop door and in sailed the old hag, her shawl drenched by the rain.

Banging on the counter, again she shrilly demanded a dozen cookies.

Stubbornly, Boss Jan counted them out, "One, two, three, four, five, six, seven, eight, nine, ten, eleven, and twelve."

"A dozen. Give me a dozen. Here are only twelve."

20

"Twelve is a dozen," insisted Boss Jan.

"One more! I want a dozen."

"Well then, if you want another, go to the devil and get it."

The words were scarcely out of his mouth when an earsplitting crash shook the rafters, and lightning kindled the old hag's eyes as she went out the door.

If his luck had been bad before, it was worse now. Invisible hands plucked bricks from his oven and pelted him until he was blue from head to wooden shoe. His wife became deaf, his children unkempt, and his trade went elsewhere.

Almost a year had passed. Boss Jan was in despair. On the patron's day in early December, he called on Saint Nicolaus. To his surprise, the bishop appeared and warned him to be more generous in his dealings with others, keeping a heart full of charity. Then the saint vanished, and—the old woman was there in his place!

For the third time she demanded one more cookie. As the chastened baker gave it to her, she exclaimed, "The spell is broken. From this time a dozen is thirteen!"

Taking a gingerbread figure of Saint Nicolaus off the counter, she made the astonished Dutchman lay his hand upon it and promise to be more liberal in the future.

So, until thirteen new States arose from the ruins of the colonies—when the shrewd Yankees restored the original measure—a baker's dozen was thirteen.

The Singing Geese

A MARYLAND STORY

A MAN WENT OUT ONE DAY TO SHOOT SOMETHING FOR dinner. And as he was going along, he heard a sound in the air above him, and looking up, saw a great flock of geese, and they were all singing.

"*La-lee-lu, come quilla, come quilla, bung, bung, bung, quilla bung.*"

He up with his gun and shot one of the geese and it sang as it fell:

"*La-lee-lu, come quilla, come quilla, bung, bung, bung, quilla bung.*"

He took it home and told his wife to cook it for dinner, and each feather, as she picked it, flew out of the window. She put the goose in the stove, but all the time it was cooking, she could hear in muffled tones from the stove:

"*La-lee-lu, come quilla, come quilla, bung, bung, bung, quilla bung.*"

23

When the goose was cooked, she set it on the table, but as her husband picked up his knife and fork to carve it, it sang:

"*La-lee-lu, come quilla, come quilla, bung, bung, bung, quilla bung.*"

When he was about to stick the fork in the goose, there came a tremendous noise, and a whole flock of geese flew through the window singing:

"*La-lee-lu, come quilla, come quilla, bung, bung, bung, quilla bung.*"

And each one stuck a feather in the goose. Then they picked it up off the dish and all flew out of the window singing:

"*La-lee-lu, come quilla, come quilla, bung, bung, bung, quilla bung!*"

ꙮ *Old Bluebeard* ꙮ

ONE TIME THEY WAS AN OLD MAN AND WOMAN HAD three sons—Jack, Will, and Tom. Will was the oldest one, Tom he was next and Jack was the least one. The old woman and the old man died and left Jack, Will, and Tom to look after the place. They was workin' away over in the field and each took his time goin' to git dinner.

Will, he was the oldest, was first and he tried to see what a good dinner he could git up. He hung the meat up afore the fire to boil, and he fixed some turnips and some potatoes and fixed everything nice for his brothers, and when it was ready he went out to blow the horn— they didn't have no dinner bell in them days—and when he blowed the horn down the holler he saw an old man comin', with his beard as blue as indigo, his teeth as long as pipe stems and his thumbs tucked behind him.

And the man says, "Have ye anything to eat?"

26

Will says, "No," cuz he didn't want the old man to come in and eat up the nice dinner he'd fixed up for his brothers.

Old Bluebeard says, "Well, I'll see about it!" And he went in and eat up everything Will had cooked up.

Will had to fly around and fix up something else for his brothers. He fixed up what he could, but he couldn't fix much cuz he didn't have time. Then he went out and blowed down the holler and when his brothers come in, they says, "What in the world took you so long to fix up such a shabby dinner?"

And Will says, "Well, I fixed ye up a good dinner, but when I went out to blow for ye to come in, an old man come up the holler, with his beard as blue as indigo, his teeth as long as pipe stems and his thumbs tucked behind him. And he walked in and ate up everything I'd fixed. So I had to fly around and fix you something else."

Tom says, "Well, I know he wouldn't have eat it all up if I'd been here."

Will says, "All right, tomorrow is your day and we'll see what he does to you."

So next morning Tom put him on some meat to boil in front of the fire, and when he come in from the new ground he got him some turnips and potatoes and pumpkin, and baked him some bread, and fixed him up a good dinner. And when he went out to blow the horn he saw an old man comin' up the holler, with his beard as blue as indigo, his teeth as long as pipe stems and his thumbs tucked behind him.

And the old man said, "Have ye anything to eat?"
And Tom says, "No."
Old Bluebeard says, "Well, we'll see about that."
And he went in and eat up everything Tom had fixed except jest a little bit of pumpkin.

Tom had to fly around and git up something else for

28

his brothers, and when they come in Jack says, "Why didn't you keep him from eatin' it up?"

Tom says, "Tomorrow is your time to git dinner and see if you can keep him from it."

And Jack says, "Bedad, I will."

So next day Jack put him some meat to boil in the fireplace and got some turnips and potatoes and fixed 'em, and when he went out to blow the horn for his brothers to come in, old Bluebeard was a-comin' up the holler, with his beard as blue as indigo, his teeth as long as pipe stems and his thumbs tucked behind him.

Jack says, "Now, uncle, you jest come in and have something to eat."

Old Bluebeard says, "No, I don't want anything."

Jack says, "Yes, but you must come in and have dinner with us."

Old Bluebeard says, "No, I don't want to," and he took around the house and took out down the holler.

Jack took out down the holler after him and saw him git down a den—a hole in the ground—and when the brothers come home and Jack was gone they thought old Bluebeard had eat Jack up 'stead of his dinner. But after a while Jack come in and they says, "Jack, where you been?"

Jack says, "I been watchin' old Bluebeard, watchin' where he went to, and I watched him go down a hole in the ground and I'm goin' to foller him." So Jack took a big old bushel basket out and put a strop on it, and him and his brothers went to old Bluebeard's hole.

Will says he was a-goin' down. Jack says, "We'll take turns. Will, go first."

So Will, he climbed in the basket and they let him down in the hole, and when he shook the rope they pulled him up and asked him what he found. Will says, "Well, I went until I saw a house and then I shook the rope."

"Oh pshaw, Will, what'd you shake the rope then fer? Why didn't you find out what was in the house?"

Will says, "Well, you go in and find out."

Tom says, "All right, I will."

So he climbed in the basket and went down 'til he was on top the house and then he shook the rope and they pulled him up. When he told 'em he shook the rope when he was on top of the house, Jack says, "You're nary one no account but me."

So he went down and looked in the house and there sat the prettiest woman he ever saw in his life. And Jack says, "Oh! you're the prettiest woman I ever saw in my life and you're goin' to be my wife."

"No," she said, "Old Bluebeard'll git you. You better git out of here."

"Oh no, he won't," says Jack. "He's a good friend

30

of mine and I'm goin' to take you up and marry you."

"No," she said, "you wait 'til you get down to the next house. You won't think nothin' of me when you see *her*."

So Jack put her in the basket and shook the rope. And when she come out, Will says, "Oh! you're the prettiest woman I ever saw in my life!"

And Tom said, "Oh! you're the prettiest woman I ever saw in my life."

Jack went on down to the next house and looked in and there was the prettiest woman he ever did see; the

31

other wa'n't nothing alongside this one. Jack says, "You're the prettiest woman I ever saw and you're goin' to be my wife. My brothers can have the other one but I'm goin' to have you."

She says, "Oh no, Jack, when you go down to the other house you won't think nothin' of me."

"Yes, I will too," says Jack. "You jest come git in this basket." So he put her in the basket and shook the rope.

Then he went down to the next house and there was the prettiest woman. Jack says, "Oh! you're jest the prettiest woman I ever did see and you're goin' to be my wife. My brothers kin have the other two but you're goin' to be my wife. Come git in this basket."

But afore she was pulled up she give him a red ribbon and told him to plait it in her hair so he'd know her when she come out, and she give him a wishin' ring. Jack put her in the basket and shook the rope.

When the brothers saw her they stopped talkin' to the other two and fell in love with her right away. Tom says, "You're goin' to be my wife." Will says, "No, she's goin' to be mine." And they started fightin'.

She says, "I won't have nary one. I'm goin' to marry Jack."

They said, "No, you won't, fer we'll leave Jack down there."

32

So they pulled up the basket and they commenced to fight and left Jack down there.

Jack jest sit there and Old Bluebeard come in and walked around but he didn't give Jack nothin' to eat. Jack jest sit there, and after a while he turned the ring on his finger, seein' how he'd fell away, and said, "I wish I was in my old corner beside the fire smokin' my old chunky pipe."

And there he was, and there was the woman with the red ribbon plaited in her hair, and she said, "Oh Jack!" And they was married, and they was rich when I left there.

⊗ *Mister Honey Mouth* ⊗

A LOUISIANA FOLK TALE

ONE DAY RABBIT AND HYENA WERE ON A JOURNEY TO the seashore. Rabbit often asked Hyena to accompany him. He liked to tease his friend and to hear all the gossip which he knew.

Down at the shore, these two saw something very strange which astonished them so much that they stopped to watch and listen. An elephant and a whale were conversing together.

"Look at them," said Hyena. "They are the two largest beasts in the world, the strongest of all animals."

"Hush," said Rabbit. "Let us go nearer and listen. I want to hear what they are saying."

The elephant was speaking to the whale.

"Friend Whale, as you are the largest and strongest in the sea, and I am the largest and strongest on land, we must rule over all the beasts. As for those who will revolt against us, we shall kill them. Hear, my friend?"

34

"Yes," answered the whale. "You keep the land and I shall keep the sea."

"Come!" said Hyena. "Let us go. It will be bad for us if we're found listening to their conversation."

"Oh, I don't care," said Rabbit. "I am more cunning than they. You will see how I am going to trick them."

"No," said Hyena. "I am afraid I must go."

"Well, go, if you are so good-for-nothing and cowardly. Go quickly. I am tired of you. You are too foolish."

Hyena disappeared into a thicket. From there, he could watch but not be seen.

Rabbit found a very long, stout rope. Then he got his drum and hid it in the grass. He took one end of the rope and went to the elephant.

"Sir, you who are so strong and so good, I wish you would render me a service. You could help me out of great trouble and keep me from losing my money."

The elephant was delighted to hear such a fine compliment, and he said, "I am at your service. I am always ready to help my friends."

"Good," said Rabbit. "I have a cow which is stuck in the mud on the coast. You know that I am not strong enough to pull her out. I need your help. Take this rope in your trunk. I shall tie the other end to the cow. When you hear me beat my drum, pull hard on

35

the rope because the cow is very deep in the mud."

"That is all right," said the elephant. "I promise you I shall pull out the cow, or the rope will break."

Rabbit took the other end of the rope and ran towards the sea. He paid a pretty compliment to the whale and asked her to do him the same favor. He told her that his cow was stuck in a bayou in the woods.

Rabbit's mouth was so honeyed that no one could refuse him anything. The whale took hold of the rope and said, "When I hear the drum, I shall pull."

"Yes," said Rabbit, "begin pulling gently, and then more and more."

"You need not be afraid," said the whale, "I will pull out your cow even if the devil were to hold her."

"That is good," said Rabbit, and whispered to himself, "We are going to laugh." Then he went back to the hiding place and beat his drum.

The elephant began to pull so hard that the rope was like a bar of iron. The whale, on her side, was pulling and pulling, and yet she was coming nearer the land. She was not in as good a place for pulling as the elephant. When she saw that she was nearing the land, she beat her tail furiously and plunged headlong under the sea. The shock was so great that the elephant was dragged to the water's edge.

"What," said he, "what is the matter? That cow

must be wonderfully strong to drag me so. Let me kneel with my front feet in the mud."

Then the elephant twisted the rope round his trunk in such a manner that he pulled the whale up onto the shore. He was very much astonished to see his friend.

"What is the matter? I thought it was Rabbit's cow I was pulling!"

"Rabbit told me the same thing," said the whale. "I believe he is playing a joke on us."

"He'll pay for that!" said the elephant. "I forbid him to eat a blade of grass on land."

37

"And I will not allow him to drink a drop of water in the sea. We must watch, and the first one that sees him must not miss him."

Then Rabbit, coming by the thicket, said to Hyena, "It is time for us to leave."

"See," said Hyena, "you always get us into trouble."

"Oh, hush. I am not through with them yet."

Rabbit and Hyena went on their way and after a while they separated. When Rabbit arrived in the woods, he found a little dead deer. The hair had fallen off his skin in many places because the dogs had bitten him. Rabbit took off the deer's skin and put it on his own back. He looked exactly like a wounded deer.

"Poor little Deer, how sick you look," said the elephant when Rabbit passed limping by him.

"Oh yes, I am suffering greatly! You see it was Rabbit who poisoned me because, as you ordered, I tried to keep him from eating grass. Take care, Mr. Elephant, Rabbit has made a bargain with the devil. It will be hard on you, if you don't take care."

The elephant was very much frightened. He said, "Little Deer, you tell Rabbit that I am his best friend. Let him eat as much grass as he wants, and present my compliments to him."

A little later the deer met the whale at the water's edge.

"Poor little Deer, why are you limping so? You seem to be very sick."

"Yes, it is Rabbit's doing. Take care, friend Whale," said Rabbit and gave the whale the same story.

The whale also was frightened and said, "I want nothing to do with the devil. Please tell Rabbit to drink as much water as he wants."

The deer went his way and when he met Hyena, he took off the deer's skin and said:

"You see, I am more cunning than they are. I can play tricks on them all the time. Where I can get away with it, another will be caught!"

"You are right indeed," said Hyena.

🌊 *Mister Deer's My Riding Horse* 🌊

A NEGRO FOLK TALE FROM THE GULF COAST

WELL, ONCE UPON A TIME, WHEN MISTER RABBIT WAS young and frisky, he went a-courting Miss Fox who lived way far back in the thick woods. Mister Fox and his family were very skeery. They seldom came out of the wood except for a little walk in the clearing near the big house when the moon shone bright. So they didn't know many people besides Mister Rabbit and Mister Deer.

Mister Deer had his eyes set on Miss Fox, too. But he didn't suspicion Mister Rabbit was a-looking that way. So he kept on being just as friendly with Mister Rabbit as he ever had been.

One day Mister Rabbit called on Miss Fox, and while they were talking, Miss Fox told him what a fine gentleman she thought Mister Deer was. Mister Rabbit just threw back his head and laughed and laughed.

"What you laughing about?" Miss Fox said.

40

Mister Rabbit just laughed on and wouldn't tell her. Miss Fox kept pestering Mister Rabbit to tell her what he was laughing about and at last Mister Rabbit stopped laughing and said:

"Miss Fox, you bear me witness I didn't want to tell you, but you just made me. Miss Fox, you call Mister Deer a fine gentleman. Miss Fox, Mister Deer's my riding horse!"

Miss Fox nearly fell over in a fainting fit. She said she didn't believe it, and she wouldn't believe it until Mister Rabbit gave her the proof.

Mister Rabbit said, "Will you believe it if you see me riding past your door?"

Miss Fox said she would and she wouldn't have anything to do with Mister Deer if the story were true.

Now for some time, Mister Rabbit had been fixing up a plan to get Mister Deer out of his way. So he said, "Good evening," to Miss Fox and clipped it off to Mister Deer's house. Mister Rabbit was so friendly with Mister Deer that he didn't suspect anything.

Presently Mister Rabbit just fell over double in his chair and groaned and moaned and Mister Deer said:

"What's the matter, Mister Rabbit? Are you sick?"

But Mister Rabbit just groaned. Then Mister Rabbit fell off the chair and rolled on the floor, and Mister Deer said:

"What ails you, Mister Rabbit?"

And Mister Rabbit groaned out, "Oh, Mister Deer, I'm dying. Take me home; take me home."

Mister Deer was mighty kindhearted and said, "Get up on my back and I'll tote you home."

But Mister Rabbit said, "Oh, Mister Deer, I'm so sick, I can't sit on your back 'less you put a saddle on."

So Mister Deer put on a saddle.

Mister Rabbit said, "I can't steady myself 'less you put my feet in the stirrups."

So Mister Deer put his feet in the stirrups.

"Oh, Mister Deer, I can't hold on 'less you put on a bridle."

So Mister Deer put on a bridle.

"Oh, Mister Deer, I don't feel right 'less I have a whip in my hand."

So Mister Deer put a whip in his hand.

"Now I'm ready, Mister Deer," said Mister Rabbit, "but go mighty easy, for I'm likely to die any minute. Please take the short cut through the woods, Mister Deer, so I can get home soon."

So Mister Deer took the short cut and forgot that it took him past Miss Fox's house. Just as he remembered, and was about to turn back, Mister Rabbit, who had slipped on a pair of spurs unbeknown to him, stuck them into his sides. At the same time he laid on the whip so that poor Mister Deer was crazy with pain and ran as fast as his legs could carry him right by the gallery where Miss Fox was standing, wide-eyed in surprise.

Mister Rabbit was up in his stirrups hollering, "Didn't I tell you Mister Deer's my riding horse!"

But after a while Miss Fox found out about Mister Rabbit's trick on Mister Deer. And she wouldn't have anything more to do with Mister Rabbit.

❧ *The Coyote and the Bear* ❧

A PUEBLO INDIAN STORY FROM NEW MEXICO

ONCE UPON A TIME KO-ÍD-DEH, THE BEAR, AND TOO-wháy-deh, the coyote, chanced to meet at a certain spot and sat down to talk. After a while the bear said:

"Friend Coyote, do you see what good land this is here? What do you say if we farm it together, sharing our labor and the crop?"

The coyote thought well of it, and said so; and after talking, they agreed to plant potatoes in partnership.

"Now," said the bear, "I have thought of a good way to divide the crop. I will take all that grows below the ground, and you take all that grows above it. Then each can take away his share when he is ready."

The coyote agreed, and when the time came they plowed the place with a sharp stick and planted their potatoes. All summer they worked together in the field, hoeing down the weeds with stone hoes and letting in water now and then from the irrigating ditch.

44

When harvest-time came, the coyote went and cut off all the potato tops at the ground and carried them home,

and afterward the bear scratched out the potatoes from the ground with his big claws and took them to his house. When the coyote saw this his eyes were opened, and he said:

"But this is not fair. You have those round things which are good to eat, but what I took home we cannot eat at all, neither my wife nor I."

"But, friend Coyote," answered the bear gravely, "did we not make an agreement? Then we must stick to it like men."

The coyote could not answer, and went home; but he was not satisfied.

45

The next spring, as they met one day, the bear said:

"Come, friend Coyote, I think we ought to plant this good land again, and this time let us plant it in corn. But last year you were dissatisfied with your share, so this year we will change. You take what is below the ground for your share, and I will take only what grows above."

This seemed very fair to the coyote, and he agreed. They plowed and planted and tended the corn; and when it came harvest-time the bear gathered all the stalks and ears and carried them home. When the coyote came to dig his share, he found nothing but roots like threads, which were good for nothing. He was very much dissatisfied; but the bear reminded him of their agreement, and he could say nothing.

That winter the coyote was walking one day by the river, the Rio Grande, when he saw the bear sitting on the ice and eating a fish. The coyote was very fond of fish, and coming up, he said:

"Friend Bear, where did you get such a fat fish?"

"Oh, I broke a hole in the ice," said the bear, "and fished for it. There are many here." And he went on eating, without offering any to the coyote.

"Won't you show me how, friend?" asked the coyote, almost fainting with hunger at the smell of the fish.

"Oh, yes," said the bear. "It is very easy." And he
broke a hole in the ice with his paw. "Now, friend
Coyote, sit down and let your tail hang in the water,
and very soon you will feel a nibble. But you must not
pull it out till I tell you."

So the coyote sat down with his tail in the cold
water. Soon the ice began to form around it, and he
called:

"Friend Bear, I feel a bite! Let me pull him out."

"No, no! Not yet!" cried the bear. "Wait till he gets
a good hold, and then you will not lose him."

So the coyote waited. In a few minutes the hole was frozen solid, and his tail was fast.

"Now, friend Coyote," called the bear, "I think you have him. Pull!"

The coyote pulled with all his might but could not lift his tail from the ice, and there he was—a prisoner. While he pulled and howled, the bear shouted with laughter and rolled on the ice and ha-ha'd till his sides were sore. Then he took his fish and went home, stopping every little while to laugh at the thought of the foolish coyote.

There on the ice the coyote had to stay until a thaw liberated him, and when he got home he was very wet and cold and half starved. And from that day to this he has never forgiven the bear and will not even speak to him when they meet and the bear says, politely, "Good morning, friend Too-wháy-deh."

❧ *The Cat, the Cock and the Lamb* ❧

A NEW MEXICAN STORY

ONCE UPON A TIME AN OLD MAN AND AN OLD WOMAN were bringing up a cock, a cat and a lamb in their house, and they loved these animals as if they were their own children. Now it happened that the old man killed a hog which he had fattened for his wife and himself to eat. When a fiesta day arrived, the old woman made fritters steeped in honey and put the meat to cook. Then she ordered the cat to guard the meat pot, the cock to fetch water and the lamb to search for fire-wood, while she and the old man went to Mass.

So, while the old people were at church, the cat took care of the meat pot; but when the cock and the lamb brought back the water and the firewood, they found the cat licking her paws. She had tasted the meat in the pot. The cock and the lamb were hungry and they wanted a taste too, but when they'd finished their bite, the cat said, "Let's go ahead and eat all of it!"

49

The three of them ate up all the meat the old woman had put to cook in the pot.

Then said the cat, "Now I am going to run away so that I won't be beaten to death when the old woman and the old man return."

"Well, then, I am going too," said the cock.

"And I also," said the lamb.

So the three animals ran off before the old people came back from Mass. They made their way over a wooded hill until they came to a very tall pine beside the entrance to a wolves' cave. The cat and the cock climbed into the pine while the lamb stayed on the ground beneath the tree.

"Climb," said the cock to the lamb. "You should be up here too!"

"Take hold of me," said the cat.

The lamb took hold of the cat and pulled himself up onto a branch. In a few moments the animals heard a noise in the cave. Then the lamb was seized with a desire to shake the dust from his fleece.

"Friends," he said, "I am going to shake my woolly coat."

"Hold tight to the branch then and shake," said the cat.

But when the lamb shook himself, he lost his balance and fell from the pine just as one of the wolves ran out of the cave. The wolf sprang at the lamb. Then the cat jumped from the tree onto the wolf's neck and began to claw his head. Half blinded, the wolf rushed back into the cave with the cat still riding on top of him.

The second wolf appeared and the cat scratched him too, while the lamb butted and the cock crowed:

Cock-a-doodle-doo! Hang them here for me!
Cock-a-doodle-doo! Hang them here for me!
Cock-a-doodle-doo!

The wolves started running for the mountains so fast you couldn't have seen even the dust behind them.

The cat, the cock and the lamb took possession of the cave, and as the wolves had left a great deal of meat, the three began to feast.

When the old man and the old woman returned from Mass, they found neither the cat, the cock nor the lamb. They couldn't imagine where they were. But when they saw there was no meat left in the pot, they suspected that the animals had eaten their dinner and then run away.

In the meantime the wolves remembered the meat they had left in the cave and they said to each other, "Let's get it and bring it to our new home."

At nightfall, the three little animals had climbed back up in the pine, so when the wolves returned they saw no one about.

Then the first wolf, after looking in the cave, said to the other, "I don't know where they are, the little man with the four sharp pocketknives, nor the obstinate big-headed person who knocked us down with a single butt, nor that noisy braggart!"

The second wolf said, "Let's go in."

And the moment they went in, the cat sprang from her branch and the lamb from his. The cat scratched furiously while the lamb butted the wolves back into the cave whenever they tried to leave. Finally the cat and the lamb grew tired of their sport, and the cock was hoarse from crowing, so they allowed the wolves to get away. This time they did not return.

The three little animals took the meat and started for the house of the old people. It was night when they reached home.

The cat said to the cock, "You climb up in that window and I'll climb up in this one."

And to the lamb she said, "You stand in front of the door and when I say 'meow,' butt!"

"And you," she said to the cock, "begin to crow."

So they took their places and when the cat gave the signal, the lamb butted the door and the cock crowed.

The old man and the old woman heard them and rushed out exclaiming, "Our animals! They have come back! They have come home!"

The old people asked the cat, the lamb and the cock where they had been. The animals told them of their adventures, and then, because they were all so happy to be together, they began to prepare for the next fiesta day.

❧ *The Old Woman and the Bear* ❧

A FOLK TALE FROM CALIFORNIA

AN OLD WOMAN SAT OUT ON THE PORCH IN HER ROCK-
ing chair all alone and smoked her pipe. She said, "Who
is going to spend this long lonesome night with me?"

A bear answered, "Me, by the corral."

So the old woman smoked her pipe and smoked her
pipe and again said, "Who is going to spend this long
lonesome night with me?"

And the bear answered, "Me, by the brush pile."

The old woman smoked her pipe and smoked her
pipe and said a third time, "Who is going to spend this
long lonesome night with me?"

And the bear answered, "Me, by the chimney
corner."

And he jumped out and ate her up!

🐚 *The Indian Shinny Game* 🐚

A STORY FROM THE SAN JOAQUIN VALLEY

"WHERE DOES THE BEST GAMBLER LIVE?" THE PRAIRIE falcon, Mih-Kit-Tee, asked his grandmother.

"Mih-Kit-Tee, you should not gamble."

"But do you know the best gambler?"

"Yes, Mih-Kit-Tee."

"Who is he?"

"Coo-Choon, the crow. No one in the world wins from him."

"Grandmother, I am going to find Crow and play with him. If he wins, he can do anything he wants with me. If I win, I will put him in the fire so that he won't gamble any more. What game does he play?"

"He plays the shinny game. He has one shinny ball, one shinny club. You have a ball and club. You start at the goal hole and knock your balls with your clubs as fast as you can over the course, around a tree or a hill and back. The first one to cover the course

56

and hit his ball back into the goal hole is the winner. That is the Indian shinny game. Crow runs fast. He will beat you."

Mih-Kit-Tee was not to be discouraged. He hung a string of eagle-down on the branch of a tree and told his grandmother, "If that string stays up until I get back, you'll know I've won. If it falls, that will be a sign I've lost."

Mih-Kit-Tee rested a while and ate Indian medicine. Then, touching the winnowing tray for good luck, he left camp.

To get ready for Crow, he raced and won from all the good runners. In the evening, he challenged Canvasback Duck. They started at the North Star and crossed the sky to the other end of the world. Farther and farther, faster and faster they flew until the sky was ribboned with the grey-white down from their bodies, but Mih-Kit-Tee won again. The place where they raced may still be seen in the sky every night. Some people call it the Milky Way.

When Mih-Kit-Tee saw that Fox had no tongue, Ground Owl only one leg, Cottontail but one ear, Antelope just one eye, and Coyote no tail, he asked, "What happened to all these people?"

They answered, "We gambled with Crow, and he won from us, our tails, our tongues, our legs, our ears."

57

"Listen, Coyote," said Mih-Kit-Tee, "I am going to play shinny with Crow. If I beat him, I am going to build a big fire and throw him in. There'll be no more gambling. Then you will get back the things you lost. I don't eat acorn mush like you. I eat Indian medicine. Come with me, Coyote, and when they give me something to eat, sit near me, and eat my portion of Crow's food. Then no one will know that I eat only Indian medicine."

So Mih-Kit-Tee and Coyote traveled together to the village where Crow lived. Crow saw them coming and he called for acorn mush and meat.

"Heh-deh, Mr. Mih-Kit-Tee."

"Heh-deh, Mr. Crow. I've come to play shinny with you."

"I'll play shinny with you, Mr. Mih-Kit-Tee, but first we have to eat."

Everyone except Mih-Kit-Tee began to eat. Nobody saw him giving his food to Coyote while he ate a little of his Indian medicine.

When everyone had finished, Crow offered Mih-Kit-Tee a shinny ball and club. Mih-Kit-Tee said that he would use his own ball and club.

On top of Sawtooth Mountain back of Mineral King was a big rock with a hole where water stood almost all summer. That was the starting place. The course lay

down the mountains, across the San Joaquin Valley, around the little hills south of Coalinga and back up to the hole on Sawtooth. The winner could do anything he wanted with the one who lost.

Mih-Kit-Tee and Crow went up on top of the Big Rock. Every one who had gambled with Crow was watching, silently. Mih-Kit-Tee hit his leg with his hand and said, "Here, my club!" His shinny club fell out of his leg onto the ground. Then he hit his ankle with his club and said, "Here, my ball!" and his shinny ball fell out of his ankle onto the ground.

When the people saw this, they looked at each other and wondered if Mih-Kit-Tee were going to win. Crow was angry, but he could not stop Mih-Kit-Tee. A player had the right to use any club and ball he could get in any way; that was part of the game.

When Crow and Mih-Kit-Tee were both ready, the coyote howled. That was the signal to start. They hit their shinny balls and were off like a pair of shooting stars. Down the south side of the river they dashed to Tulare Lake, over the water to two pointed hills south of Coalinga, around the hills; then they started back. Mih-Kit-Tee was almost up with Crow when Crow thought, "Now I must get way ahead." So hitting his ball with great skill, he ran swiftly after it and soon was out of sight.

Then said Mih-Kit-Tee to himself, "Crow might win! I must stop him. Come on, bog, help me beat him."

Suddenly, Crow's shinny ball fell into a boggy trap. Crow swung his club once, twice, many times. He could not free his ball.

Mih-Kit-Tee ran on and when he reached Tulare, he said, "I'm well ahead of Crow now. Bog, give him back his ball." Then the boggy place gave up the ball and Crow came on like a mad hornet. On his way to a grove of oak trees, he passed Mih-Kit-Tee once again.

"That Crow is going to win anyway. Oak trees, help me out," begged Mih-Kit-Tee.

Crow's shinny ball hit an oak and all of the oak balls fell to the ground. Crow couldn't tell which was his.

60

He ran round and round, searching for his shinny ball.

Mih-Kit-Tee passed Crow and went on as fast as he could, far ahead. Finally he said, "Oak trees, let Crow have his ball."

Crow's ball rolled out where he could see it. He hit hard and for the third time left his opponent behind.

Then Mih-Kit-Tee thought Crow surely would win. "There's one last chance," he said. "Come on, fog, help me now."

So the fog came down and hid Crow's ball. Mih-Kit-Tee passed him, then said, "Well, fog, let Crow have his ball."

When the fog cleared, Crow caught up with Mih-Kit-Tee who was waiting for him to place his final shot.

"First here, first shoot," said Crow.

Carefully, Mih-Kit-Tee aimed and dropped his ball straight into the goal hole. All the people who had been watching the game shouted and whooped.

When Crow hit his ball, he sliced into the pile of earth under it. The ball stopped short of the goal. Crow squatted down on the ground and took root like an oak tree. Mih-Kit-Tee began to build a big fire.

Then Crow said, "Mih-Kit-Tee, I have two sisters. They are the prize for this shinny game. I am giving them to you."

"No, Crow. I want you, not your sisters. I am going to throw you into this fire so that these people will get back everything they lost to you."

Crow spoke again, "I have a house full of Indian money. That will be a fine prize for winning this shinny game."

"No, Crow. Your money is not you."

Mih-Kit-Tee did not know that Crow had grown roots. He took hold of Crow's arms and pulled and pulled. Then Heron tried and Coyote, Elk, and many others, but no one could get Crow loose.

Finally Mih-Kit-Tee said, "We can't move him. We'll have to send for Bear. He is strong. He will be able to throw him in the fire. Dove, go and tell Bear to come and help."

So Dove went to the cave where Bear lived.

"Heh-deh, Mr. Bear."

"Heh-deh, Mr. Dove. What brings you here?"

"Mr. Mih-Kit-Tee beat Crow playing the shinny game. He wants to throw Crow in the fire and make an end of gambling, but no one can move Crow. You are strong. Will you come and throw him in for us?"

"Yes, Mr. Dove, I'll come."

Dove ran back as fast as he could go. Bear came jouncing after him. "I can pull him up," he assured Mih-Kit-Tee. He stood right behind Crow, caught his

62

arms around him and pulled and growled and growled and pulled, but Crow did not move.

After a while Bear said, "Why don't you make the fire on top of him?"

"No," said Mih-Kit-Tee, "if we leave one little piece of him on the ground, people will not get back the things they have lost."

Then Mih-Kit-Tee called Road-runner. "Go tell Mountain Lion about our trouble. He is another strong one."

Road-runner went to the home of Mountain Lion. "Heh-deh, Mr. Mountain Lion."

"Heh-deh, Mr. Road-runner."

"Mr. Mih-Kit-Tee sent me to get you. He won Crow playing the shinny game. He wants to throw him in the fire but none of our people can move him."

"All right, Mr. Road-runner. I can move him."

So Road-runner ran back as fast as his legs would carry him. Mountain Lion came leaping after him to the place where Crow sat. Mountain Lion caught his arms around Crow and pulled and scratched and scratched and pulled, but Crow did not move.

Then catching his hands under Crow's neck, Mountain Lion pulled him back as far as he could, held him there and wondered why he wouldn't come up. Then he looked under Crow and saw the roots, like an oak's, tying him to the ground. Mountain Lion thought hard.

"Like a tree, this fellow has roots! I'll have to be smart to get him loose," said Mountain Lion as he leaped in front of Crow and put his arms under Crow's arms.

After one hard quick pull, Mountain Lion worked Crow round and round in a circle and soon the roots came loose. He threw Crow into the fire and in that moment Mih-Kit-Tee saw that once again Coyote had his tail; Antelope, his eye; Fox, his tongue; Groundhog, his leg; Cottontail, his ear; Blackbird, his wing; Woodpecker, his beak and Badger, his claws.

Crow had played his last game of Indian shinny.

⊗ *Coyote and the Alder Stump* ⊗

A WINTU TALE FROM CALIFORNIA

OLD COYOTE WAS COMING DOWN THE RIVER, COMING down south. He had had enough of the snow around Shasta; he was tired of that glistening world of white and blue. Down the river he was coming, down to meet the spring.

With each day's journey, the sun grew stronger, baring more of the brown earth, warming the leafless trees. Then one morning Coyote felt a lilt in the air.

"My, I feel fine," he said out loud. "I could lick anything today."

Just then Coyote came to an old alder stump. He took a deep breath and struck at the stump. His right arm went in; he could not get it loose. He struck again and his left arm went in. Then he kicked with his right foot and that went in; then he kicked and caught his left foot. In a rage he bumped his head and that went

65

in too. Then he lay there wondering how in the world he was going to get out.

Finally Coyote heard a bird light on top of the stump. It was Woodcock. Then Woodcock went to work pecking. He pecked and pecked and at last Old Coyote was free. And when Coyote got out, "Oh, little nephew," he said, "I've been asleep."

And that was all.

☒ *The Treasure of Tacoma* ☒

AN INDIAN STORY FROM WASHINGTON STATE

MANY YEARS AGO, UNDER THE SHADOW OF MOUNT Tacoma, lived an old man of the Squallyamish. This Indian knew every quiet salmon pool, every secluded elk trail in all the forest, but he loved only hiaqua, those small opaque shells which his people used for money. He wanted to be the richest man in his tribe.

Always fishing and hunting, the old man supplied his lazy friends with salmon and dried elk meat in return for hiaqua. He took no part in their games and feasts. He never gave his squaw a string of shells for a necklace. Often he wondered, as he fished some lonely stream, whether his guardian spirit would help him find more hiaqua.

One dancing fall day as he walked in the forest he seemed to hear a voice asking, "Are you brave? Dare you go to the cave where my treasure is hid?"

"I dare," said the old man out loud.

67

"I dare," echoed back from the great rocks and snowy wastes of Mount Tacoma.

"Listen," the voice whispered and the old man gave ear while his guardian, the Elk Spirit, told him where a wealth of hiaqua lay buried.

When the cry of a jay broke the spell, the old man started home to make his preparations. For the guardian spirits will never do for a man what he can do for himself.

After sending his curious squaw to gather kamas roots, he took a pair of enormous elk-horns and made from each horn a two-pronged spade. He packed kippered salmon and kamas and filled his pouch with kinnikinnick to smoke in his black stone pipe. With bow, arrows, and elk-horn spades on his back, he set out in the gathering dusk. Back from her forage, his squaw watched him disappear up a trail.

All that night and the next day he followed familiar paths. Elk and deer bounding through the trees passed him by. Salmon he left undisturbed in their streams. The second night he camped just below the great snows of Tacoma. The wind off the mountain chilled him but he made no fire for fear of being discovered by some hunter. When the moon rose, he took to his path again.

Looking scarcely to right or left he went on through

68

the paling moonlight until dawn found him at Tacoma's summit. There, within a great hollow bordered by the whitest of snow, lay a black lake in a well of purple rock.

On a ledge at the eastern end of the lake stood three stone monuments. As the sun glinted these towering sentinels, the old man made his way to the first giant stone. Its top was shaped like a salmon's head. He turned to the second, its top an image of the kamas bulb. He hastened to the third. It resembled an elk's head as it appears in early summer with antlers sprouting under their rough jacket of velvet. Since Elk was his guardian spirit, he regarded this third stone as a sign of good fortune. Laying down his pack and unwrapping his spades, he began to dig in the frozen snow.

Hardly had he struck his first blow when he heard behind him a sudden puff. Turning round he saw a huge otter, twice as large as any he had ever seen, clambering over the edge of the lake. The animal paused and hit the snow with his tail, whereupon otter after otter appeared until twelve had climbed out of the lake. Following their chief, they made a solemn circle around the old man. Then the chief otter jumped to the top of the elk-head stone and seated himself between the horns. Together, they gave another mighty puff.

The old man paused. Never had he seen such otters,

69

but remembering the promise of hiaqua, he began digging again. At every thirteenth stroke of his spade, the chief otter tapped his tail on the monument; the others tapped theirs on the snow.

Tired, the old man paused to catch his breath. Straightway the chief otter turned and, swinging his tail, gave the weary digger a thump on the shoulder. Then the whole band smote him with their tails until he returned to work.

Presently, the old man broke his elk-horn spade. The

chief otter leaped down and taking the second spade in his mouth, presented it to him. Then the chief showed the broken spade to the circle of otters. These strange actions baffled the old man; nevertheless, he went on digging.

Beneath the snow, the rock lay first in plates, then in scales. Finally the scale was so thin, it cracked into flakes as he turned it over. Under it was a large square hole.

It was filled to the brim with hiaqua!

The old man was rich beyond his greatest hopes. He thrust his arm into the pit. He could not feel the bottom. There were countless hundreds of the precious shells.

The hiaqua was strung on long, stout, elk sinews. Four of these strings he wound around his waist. Three, he hung across each shoulder. Five, he took in each hand. Twenty strings of pure white hiaqua, every shell large, smooth, unbroken, beautiful! He could carry no more. He put down his burden while he covered the still-full pit with the scale stones and brushed snow across its top.

Gloating over his wealth, the old man forgot to thank the Elk Spirt. He left no hiaqua in token of gratitude on the great stones. Without one gesture of appreciation, he picked up the strings of shells and began his climb to the crater's edge.

All at once the otters, with a mighty puff, plunged one by one into the black lake and beat the water with their tails. The old man could hear the splashing as

he struggled through the snow. When he reached the rim, he looked back and saw a thick mist over the lake's center and under the mist a black cloud filled with the spirits of the place. The wind howled and the sky grew dark.

Hastily the old man stepped from the crater's edge and started down his trail. He had not gone a bow's length when the storm threw him to the ground. Clutching his strings of hiaqua, he listened to the rising wail of the spirits:

"*Ha, ha, hiaqua. Ha, ha, ha!*"

Each time the old man got to his feet the gale tossed him into another snowbank. At last he determined to make an offering to the spirits. Into the whirlwind, he threw his left handful, five strings of precious hiaqua.

There was a lull, and then the storm began anew—black, louder, harsher than before—and the voices shrilled again:

"*Ha, ha, hiaqua. Ha, ha, ha!*"

Terrified, he flung away the shells, string after string. Each time there was only a moment's silence, followed by a puff from the invisible otters, before the storm renewed its fury. As the last string swirled into the darkening night, he fell exhausted on a deep snowbank.

. . . . . .

There had never been a fresher morning, thought the old man when he woke. Lying on the very spot from which he had started to climb the crater, he heard a jay greet the rising sun. Hungry, he felt for his bag of kamas roots and smoke leaf pouch. By his side were the elk-sinew bag strings and the black stone pipe, but no bag, no kamas, no kinni-kinnick. All around him were kamas plants, strangely out of place on a mountainside, and overhead was a large arbutus tree with glistening leaves, ripe for smoking.

73

The old man found his hardwood sticks under the grass. He kindled a fire and while some kamas was roasting, he laid arbutus leaves to dry on a flat stone.

After eating breakfast, he realized he was no longer bruised, just very stiff as if he had not walked in a long time. Chasing off a bluebird who wanted to perch on his head, he felt his hair. It was matted and reached way down his back.

Quietly he sat smoking his pipe and looking up at Mount Tacoma. He was calm and content. Hiaqua no longer crowded his mind. Instead, he found a longing in his heart to see his people.

The old man got up and started down the mountain. The woods seemed strangely changed. Moss-covered firs and cedars lay across his old trail. Coming at sunset to the clearing where his lodge had stood, he was surprised to see a new and larger lodge in its place.

Nearby a very old squaw, decked with strings of hiaqua and costly beads, was tending a kettle of salmon over an open fire. She resembled his own squaw as an ancient smoked salmon is like a newly dried one. He listened to her lonely song.

> My old man has gone, gone, gone,
> My old man to Tacoma has gone.
> To hunt the elk, he went long ago,
> When will he come down, down, down,
> Down to the salmon-pot and me?

Realizing who she was, the old man ran to greet his faithful squaw.

> He has come from Tacoma,
> Down, down, down,
> Down to the salmon-pot ánd you!

Asleep on the mountain, he had been gone many years. His squaw had waited for his return and lived by trading herbs and kamas bulbs. The new lodge and necklaces were signs of her success.

The tribe, as well as his squaw, soon learned that the old man who had awakened to a changed world was changed too within himself. He no longer thought only of hiaqua. He wanted to feast with his friends, to share with them the salmon pools, the hidden elk lanes, all his forest lore. And in his new-found wisdom, he became the great medicine man of the Squallyamish.

🦋 *Stealing the Springtime* 🦋

AN INDIAN STORY FROM THE NORTHWEST

"THE SNOWS WILL SOON COME," SAID TWO-COMES-over-the-hill, looking gravely at the sparkling lodge-fire. "But the Winter does not last as it once did. I will tell you why. Of course Skinkoots, the Coyote, had a hand in what happened to change the Seasons. It was Skinkoots who started it all. And we are glad he did, for now the Summer stays with us six Moons.

"Listen! The snow was deep. It bent the trees. It covered the ice on the lakes until they looked like parks in the forest. Every Person was thin, even those who store up food for the Winter. The busiest of these could not gather enough food during the short Summer to last him through the long Winter.

"Skinkoots was walking on his snow-shoes. He was hungry, and asked at every lodge for something to eat. At last he came to the lodge of an Old Woman. This Old Woman was the Pine Squirrel-person, and she gave

76

him some food. The food was wild-rose hips which she had gathered during the Summer-time. She did not have many left, and she cried when Skinkoots ate the last one.

" 'Oh, dear, what can I do? It will not be Spring for a long time. I shall die!' she wailed.

" 'What is that you are saying?' asked Skinkoots, licking his chops.

" 'I said there is no more food and it is Winter. I shall starve. Oh, what shall I do?'

" 'Do? Why, cry, of course! Cry hard! And when the Persons come here and ask you why you cry, do

77

not answer them. Just keep on crying. Finally I will come in and ask: "Do you say there will be no more food for a long time?" And you must say: "Yes." '

"Skinkoots went out of the lodge and the Old Woman began to cry. Persons came to her lodge and asked: 'Why do you cry?' But she would not answer them. She just kept on crying, crying, crying, until in came Skinkoots.

" 'What is going on here?' he asked of all the Persons there.

" 'This Old Woman is crying, and she will not tell us why she cries. That is all,' answered somebody, across the fire.

" 'Say, you,' said Skinkoots, looking at the Old Woman, 'do you say there will be no more food until Spring?'

" 'Yes,' wailed the Old Woman, 'that is what I said. What shall we do to bring back the Springtime?'

" 'Well, I will see about this,' said Skinkoots, and went out of the Old Woman's lodge.

"There was a village of many lodges. It was far away and strong. The Persons who lived there kept the Summer-time tied up in a Moose-skin bag. They kept all the Seasons that way. They used to untie the Winter and let him stay out twelve months sometimes. This was because they liked him best. But so much Winter made it hard for the other Persons, and something had to be done about it.

"Skinkoots knew about all this, and he traveled steadily until he had found the Softest-walker, and the Farthest-thrower, and the Strongest-one among all the Persons he knew. He said to them: 'The Springtime is in a Moose-skin bag that hangs in the Chief's lodge over that way.' And he pointed North. 'Let us go and steal that bag and untie it. But we must not get hold of the wrong one, for there are three bags hanging there. We must steal the bag that holds the Springtime and not make a mistake, or we shall mix things.'

" 'Good,' said the Grizzly Bear. 'I shall have a hard time traveling. I am so sleepy and heavy. But I will help you. Lead on.'

" 'Yes,' said Skinkoots, 'you are the Strongest-person. Your Medicine is powerful. Come with us.'

"And so these four started for the strange village. All the other Persons followed to learn what was going on.

"At last they came to the village. It was nearly hidden by the deep snow, and looked bad under the stars.

" 'Hey, you Persons, hide yourselves on that hill,' said Skinkoots, beckoning the Grizzly Bear and the Softest-walker and the Farthest-thrower to come to him.

" 'See that big lodge?' asked Skinkoots, pointing to

79

a big black tepee with white smoke coming from its top.

" 'Yes, we see it,' said the Grizzly Bear and the Softest-walker and the Farthest-thrower, craning their necks and pricking up their ears.

" 'Well, that is it,' said Skinkoots, and you must be careful. Listen! There will be an Old Woman in that lodge. She is a loud talker, and you must be careful not to let her talk much, Remember this.

" 'Here, Softest-walker, take this pitch, and when you get inside sit by the lodge-fire and pretend to warm your hands, but melt the pitch; melt the pitch in your hand. When the pitch is soft and very sticky you must ask: "Where is the Springtime, Old Woman?"

" 'She will say, "It is hanging there," and point to the bag. Then you must stop her mouth with the hot pitch and hold it there until it sticks *tight*. Then the Old Woman will not be able to speak. The hot pitch will stop her words. When you have done this, take down the bag that holds the Springtime and throw it outside. Have you listened?'

" 'Yes,' answered Softest-walker, 'I have listened.'

" 'Now *you*, Farthest-thrower, listen to me,' said Skinkoots, speaking fast. 'When this Person throws that bag outside the lodge, you grab it. Grab it quick! And throw it far; farther than you ever threw a thing

80

before. Throw it over that way.' And he pointed to the hill where the other Persons were hiding. 'Well, that is your job,' said Skinkoots. 'Have you listened, Far-thest-thrower?'

" 'Yes,' answered Farthest-thrower, 'I have listened.'

" 'And now *you*, Strongest-one,' he said to the Grizzly Bear, 'go over there on that hill among the others. When the bag comes you catch it. Catch it and *tear* it. Tear it *quickly!* That is all you have to do. Have you listened, Strongest-one?'

" 'Yes,' answered Grizzly Bear-person, 'I have lis-tened.'

" 'Well, then get at your jobs. I will be over there to watch what is going on. Now be careful, all of you. And remember my words!'

"Softest-walker went to the lodge and slipped in-side with the ball of pitch in his hand. He did not make a sound in his walking.

"Farthest-thrower sat down on the snow piled up by the door. He could hear all that went on inside, too. And he listened.

"Softest-walker sat down by the fire and held his hands over it. Yes, he held them where the ball of pitch would get hot.

" 'The weather is cold, Old Woman,' he said, look-ing up at the three bags hanging on the lodge-poles.

81

" 'Yes, it is,' she answered, without even looking at him.

"The pitch was growing soft now. It was pretty sticky already, so Softest-walker asked: 'Where is the Springtime, Old Woman?'

" 'That is it, hanging over your head,' she answered, pointing to the bag.

"Swow! Softest-walker stopped the Old Woman's mouth with the hot pitch, and held it there!

"Oh, ho! She tried to speak! She tried to scream! But the hot pitch stuck tight and held back her words, just as Skinkoots had said it would. She tried to run

outside, but Softest-walker pushed her back and grabbed the bag.

"Oh, ho! He grabbed the bag! The Old Woman threw her arms around him, but he managed to shake her off, and toss the bag out through the door, where Strongest-thrower was waiting for it.

"Oh, ho! He grabbed it! Lifted it high and threw it! Up—up it went, and over the other lodges.

"Both Softest-walker and Farthest-thrower saw it sail to the hill as they ran away after it. They saw Grizzly Bear catch the bag and tear it open, felt the soft Winds touching their faces, even before they reached their friends on the hillside. Oh, ho! It was *Springtime!*

"The snow was melting by the time Softest-walker and Farthest-thrower caught up with the other Persons, who were running away with the Springtime.

"Ho!"

❧ *Little Bear* ❦

AN INDIAN STORY FROM WISCONSIN

ONCE AN OLD MAN AND AN OLD WOMAN HAD THREE daughters and the youngest was a little bear.

The two older daughters set out one day to seek their fortunes. After traveling for a while, they looked around and saw the little bear overtaking them. They did not want the company of their younger sister so they took her home and tied her to the doorposts of the wigwam. Then off they went again.

Silently they made their way through the trees until a rustling branch warned that the little bear a second time was following them, the doorposts on her back. The older sisters untied the posts and bound her to a huge rock. Then they continued on their journey.

Soon they came to a river too deep to cross. As they stood watching the water, up came their younger sister with the huge rock on her shoulders. They loosened the rock, threw it into the middle of the river, laid a pine tree on it and walked across to the far side.

This time the little bear went with them.

After a long journey, the three came to a wigwam where an old woman lived with her two daughters. The old woman asked where they were going. To seek their fortunes, they replied. She invited them in, gave them supper, and the two older sisters went to sleep in the same bed with the old woman's daughters.

But the little bear chose to sit by the fire telling stories to the old woman. At last both she and her listener appeared to fall asleep. Through her eyelashes, the little bear watched the old woman take a long knife from its cover and start polishing it. Just then, the little bear sneezed. The old woman quickly put away her knife. The little bear pretended to go back to sleep while the old woman edged nearer the fire and dozed off. On tiptoe the little bear woke her sisters and they hastened from the wigwam.

In the morning when the old woman awoke and saw that her three guests had left, she was very angry. She jumped up into the sky and tore down the sun. Hiding it in her wigwam, she hoped the little bear and her sisters would get lost in the dark. But they journeyed on and soon met a man carrying a light. He said he was searching for the sun. Then they came to a large village where all of the men were carrying lights.

85

Their chief was sick because the sun had vanished, and the days were dark without its glory.

When the chief was told about the three sisters and that the youngest was a little bear, he knew she must be someone special. So the chief asked the little bear whether she could bring back the sun.

"Yes," she answered. "Give me two handfuls of maple sugar and your eldest son."

Taking the maple sugar, she went to the wigwam of the old woman, climbed to the top, and tossed the sugar

86

through a hole into a kettle of wild rice which the old woman was cooking. When the old woman tasted the rice, she found it too sweet, so she went out after water to put in the kettle. The little bear jumped down, ran into the wigwam, grabbed the hidden sun and threw it skyward.

When the little bear returned to the village, she gave the chief's eldest son to her eldest sister for a husband.

The old woman was angry, very angry, to see the sun again in the sky, so she jumped up and tore down the moon. The good old chief again became sick because the nights were all dark. He asked the little bear whether she could bring back the moon.

"Yes," she said, "if you give me two handfuls of salt and your next oldest son."

Taking the salt, she climbed on top of the old woman's wigwam and dropped it into her boiling kettle. Again the old woman went after water. The little bear ran into the wigwam and catching up the moon, threw it back into the sky. Then she returned to the village and gave the chief's second son to her second sister.

The old woman was angry, very angry, to see the moon again in the sky, so she jumped up and tore down the North Star. Then the chief was sick at heart because his trappers and rice gatherers needed their ancient guide. So again he called on the little bear.

"Give me two handfuls of maple sugar and your youngest son," she answered. Then she went back to the old woman's wigwam and sweetening the kettle, once more sent her in search of water. The little bear ran into the wigwam, seized the North Star, and tossed it back into the sky.

But the chief did not wish to be parted so soon from his youngest son. He persuaded the little bear to look for a horse with a collar of bells, a favorite long missing from his band.

Again the little bear went to the old woman's wigwam and, doing as she had done before, stepped inside. There was the chief's horse. She had slipped his collar almost off when, at the tinkle of a bell, the old woman came running. She grabbed the little bear by the scuff of the neck and stuffed her into a bag which she hung high on a tree. Then the old woman went to the woods in search of a whipping stick.

The little bear bit a hole in the bag, climbed down and silently removed the horse's collar. Losing no time, she led the chief's horse back to the village.

When the little bear returned to the chief, he gave her his youngest son for a husband. But the young man was very unhappy because his wife was a bear, so one night the little bear told her husband to throw her into the fire. Hesitantly, he obeyed her command. Then, in the flickering light, he was amazed to see a beautiful young woman step from the flames.

After that, the chief's youngest son lived with his bride many golden summers. She was still called "Little Bear."

❧ *About the Stories in This Book* ❧

In America there are many stories which echo Old World tales. Often the plots were brought by early colonists, then told and told again until the tales were reborn in their new country. Sometimes the likeness between the stories from distantly separated lands remains a puzzle, the only apparent answer the fact that people everywhere love to laugh, to seek adventure, to dream dreams.

Folk-lore societies and journals refer to the person who first writes down or otherwise permanently records a tale in a particular version as the "recorder."

The recorder of "With a Wig, With a Wag," first heard it about 1827 from a schoolmate in Littleton, Massachusetts. It is reminiscent of "The Old Witch" in Joseph Jacobs' *More English Fairy Tales*.

There have been Norse, German and Irish versions of the story here called "Rusty Jack." In the Irish version, as told by Yeats in *Irish Fairy and Folk Tales*, the talking crow is a talking magpie. "Rusty Jack" was recorded after it was told in New York State in 1912 by Della Miller who had learned it from hearing her mother tell it at storytelling bees.

In "A Dozen Is Thirteen" the climax of the story takes place on St. Nicholas, or, as the Dutch say, St. Nicolaus Day, December 6. To the early Dutch settlers St. Nicolaus was a favorite. In New Amsterdam, they named their first church in his honor. Generous St. Nicolaus, shortened to Santa Klaus, was the predecessor of Santa Claus. Olie-kocks are rich cakes made with an unusual amount of shortening. This Dutch story is one explanation of the phrase, "a baker's dozen." Our version is a retelling of "The Baker's Dozen" in *Myths and Legends of Our Own Land*, Vol. 1, by Charles M. Skinner; J. B. Lippincott Company, Philadelphia, 1896.

There is no indication of the origin of "The Singing Geese." People from many countries settled the shores of Maryland, and this story might have come from any of them.

"Old Bluebeard" will remind readers of "Old Fire Draga-man," one of the stories collected by Richard Chase in *The Jack Tales*. The people of our southern mountain coun-try are great storytellers, and the lazy but always-victorious boy named Jack is a favorite hero who appears in many of their stories. The stories themselves are basically English, for the mountain people are descendants of the English and have kept very much to themselves. "Old Bluebeard" was recorded first in the exact language used by the storyteller, Mrs. Jane Gentry of Hot Springs, North Carolina.

The travels of a folk tale are well illustrated by *"Mister Honey Mouth."* The story is one of a group in which the hyena is always the dupe and the rabbit always the clever one. It was given to the collector by a New Orleans Negro, Dorlis Aguillard. Originally an African story, the tale was brought to America by the Negro and was first written down in Louisiana in French!

"Mister Deer's My Riding Horse" is another Negro tale which Uncle Remus fans will recognize. This particular version was told by a Negro nurse to a Louisiana child, who remembered it for many years and finally recorded it.

In all Pueblo Indian coyote stories, the coyote is the victim of jokes and the bear is a very wise animal. This collection's "The Coyote and the Bear" comes from the Teé-wahn pueblo of Isleta in New Mexico. There is a well-known variation in which the coyote's frozen tail is left in the ice. The story was, of course, told on winter nights. "The Coyote and the Bear" is reprinted from *The Man Who Married the Moon*, by Charles F. Lummis; The Century Company, New York, 1894.

"The Cat, the Cock and the Lamb" is much like the "Bremen-town Musicians" of the Brothers Grimm. It was told to the recorder by 72-year-old Marcial Lucero of Cochití, and comes from a group collected from Spanish-speaking inhabitants of northern New Mexico, in the Rio Grande Valley. This part of America was one of the first visited by Spaniards after the conquest of Mexico, and Spanish tales have been told there ever since.

"The Old Woman and the Bear" is one of a group of English folk tales collected in California.

The Yokut Indians of California told the mythical hero story called "The Indian Shinny Game." Their shinny game was almost like our golf, except that they did not count the number of times they hit the ball, but played the game as a race to the outpost and back. Prairie Falcon's course in the story began just south of what is now Sequoia National Park, and crossed the San Joaquin Valley.

A California Wintu Indian story is "Coyote and the Alder Stump," which is similar to the Southern Negro stories of Tarbaby, and to the African story, "Wakaima and the Clay Man," by Kalibala and Davis. The Wintu, the third largest nationality of California Indians, were exceeded in numbers and land only by the Shoshoneans and the Yokuts. They lived on the west side of the Sacramento Valley.

There are many legends about the high peaks of the Pacific Coast. "The Treasure of Tacoma" was told by Hamitchou, an ancient of the Squallyamish tribe at Fort Nisqualli, Washington State, in 1853. It was not recorded until after that time. The ending, strangely enough, is very like the ending of Washington Irving's famous "Rip Van Winkle," a legend set in other mountains a continent away! Kamas is a plant with bulb-like roots which are the staple food of West Coast Indians. Our story of "The Treasure of Tacoma" is a retelling of "Hamitchou's Legend" in *The*

Canoe and the Saddle by Theodore Winthrop; Boston, Tichnor and Fields, 1863.

Skinkoots the coyote, who manages everything in "Stealing the Springtime," is a hero of the Kootenai Indians, "Flatbow people" who were enemies of the Blackfeet. Their country, some of the most magnificent in the Northwest, lies on both sides of the Canadian border from British Columbia through northern Idaho and western Montana.

There are reminders of the English "Mollie Whuppie" in the Indian story of "Little Bear." The story from which this retelling is drawn was narrated by old Pa-skin, an Ojibwa woman over a hundred years old, living on the Lac Courte Oreille Reservation in Wisconsin.